CHIMPANZEE!

by Tessa Kenan

BUMBA BOOKS™

LERNER PUBLICATIONS ◆ MINNEAPOLIS

Note to Educators:

Throughout this book, you'll find critical thinking questions. These can be used to engage young readers in thinking critically about the topic and in using the text and photos to do so.

Lerner Publications Company
A division of Lerner Publishing Group, Inc.
241 First Avenue North
Minneapolis, MN 55401 USA

For reading levels and more information, look up this title at www.lernerbooks.com.

Library of Congress Cataloging-in-Publication Data

Names: Kenan, Tessa, author.
Title: It's a chimpanzee! / by Tessa Kenan.
Other titles: It is a chimpanzee!
Description: Minneapolis : Lerner Publications, [2017] | Series: Bumba books. Rain forest animals | Audience: Age 4–8. | Audience: K to grade 3. | Includes bibliographical references and index.
Identifiers: LCCN 2016021983 (print) | LCCN 2016026866 (ebook) | ISBN 9781512425727 (lb : alk. paper) | ISBN 9781512429336 (pb : alk. paper) | ISBN 9781512427592 (eb pdf)
Subjects: LCSH: Chimpanzees—Juvenile literature. | Rain forest animals—Juvenile literature.
Classification: LCC QL737.P94 K46 2017 (print) | LCC QL737.P94 (ebook) | DDC 599.885—dc23

LC record available at https://lccn.loc.gov/2016021983

Manufactured in the United States of America
1 – VP – 12/31/16

Expand learning beyond the printed book. Download free, complementary educational resources for this book from our website, www.lernerresource.com.

Table of Contents

Chimpanzees Swing

Chimpanzees are a kind of ape.

Many of them live in rain forests.

Chimpanzees spend a lot of

time in trees.

They swing from branch to branch.

They make nests out of leaves.

Chimpanzees are almost

as big as people.

These animals usually walk

on all fours.

They can also walk

on two legs.

Hands and thumbs help

chimpanzees eat.

They eat fruit and plants.

They eat insects too.

What else might hands help these animals do?

Chimpanzees are smart.

They use tools.

This chimpanzee uses a stick

as a tool.

It digs for food.

How else might chimpanzees use tools?

Chimpanzees live

in groups.

The groups are

called communities.

Each community can

have fifty or

more chimpanzees.

Sometimes chimpanzees

get bugs on their fur.

Chimpanzees clean

one another.

They pick off the bugs.

Mother chimpanzees have one baby at a time.

The baby hangs on to its mother.

It rides on her back.

Why do you think the baby stays near its mother?

19

The young chimpanzee stays close

to its mother.

It may stay with her for ten years.

Chimpanzees can live to be

forty-five years old.

Parts of a Chimpanzee

arm

fur

thumb

hand

leg

Picture Glossary

ape

a large animal related to monkeys and humans

communities

groups of chimpanzees that live together

rain forests

thick, tropical forests where lots of rain falls

tools

things used to do a job

Index

Read More

Hansen, Grace. *Chimpanzees.* Minneapolis: Abdo Kids, 2016.

Marsico, Katie. *Chimpanzees.* Ann Arbor, MI: Cherry Lake Publishing, 2013.

Schuh, Mari. *Meet a Baby Chimpanzee.* Minneapolis: Lerner Publications, 2016.

Photo Credits

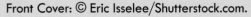